Caring Caregiver Book for Families

Help the one you love to stay in their own home - by Applying 15 Key Steps for Keeping Your Elderly Parent at Home – Safely & Comfortably

Every caring child wants to keep their elderly parent healthy, comfortable, and vibrant in their own home. They want to share memories of the past, respect their parents' wishes, and add meaningful life to the end of life.

In this revolutionary Itty Bitty® Book, **John S. Smith, Jr.** walks you through the steps and techniques for keeping your parents healthy and active at a time when they are slowing down.

Following these steps will help you prepare for challenges related to the aging process. It will serve as a companion, helping to assure that they have the paperwork needed to make sure their wishes are known and will be fulfilled.

For example:

- Documents to have on hand in anticipation of unexpected situations.
- Encouraging self-care, keeping your parent active and involved in their care in the event that you are far away from home.
- Resources available to pay for long-term care at home.

Pick up a copy of this powerful book today and experience the joys and rewards of caring for your elderly parent right in their own home.

Your Amazing Itty Bitty® Eldercare Book

15 Key Steps for Keeping Your Elderly Parent At Home – Safely & Comfortably

John S. Smith Jr., RN

Published by Itty Bitty® Publishing
A subsidiary of S & P Productions, Inc.

Copyright © 2017 John Saye Smith, Jr.

All rights reserved. No part of this book may be reproduced or transmitted in any form or by any means, electronic or mechanical, including photocopying, recording or by any information storage and retrieval system, without written permission of the publisher, except for inclusion of brief quotations in a review.

Printed in the United States of America

Itty Bitty Publishing
311 Main Street, Suite D
El Segundo, CA 90245
(310) 640-8885

ISBN: 978-0-9987597-1-5

This book is dedicated to all the caregivers who sacrifice their time, resources, and energy to care for the one they truly love.

Stop by our Itty Bitty® website to find interesting information regarding eldercare and keeping your elderly parents comfortably and safely at home.

www.IttyBittyPublishing.com

Or visit John S. Smith, Jr. RN, BSN, at

www.prestigewecare.com

Table of Contents

Introduction
- Step 1. Tough Conversation
- Step 2. Get Your Aging Parent(s) Involved
- Step 3. Gather All Important Documents
- Step 4. Get Legal
- Step 5. Getting in the Game
- Step 6. Get Help Behind the Wheel
- Step 7. Getting a Grip on the Meds
- Step 8. Encouraging Self-Care
- Step 9. Finding an Adult Day/Senior Center
- Step 10. Limiting Stress Over Distance
- Step 11. Anticipating Your Parents' Needs
- Step 12. Anticipating Cost of Care
- Step 13. Long-Term Care; Where Is the Money?
- Step 14. Adding Life to Years
- Step 15. Keep the Ability in Disability

Introduction

So many countries around the world have a tradition of caring for their aging family members. That is not a tradition in America.

As our country faces dramatic social and economic changes over the next few years, caring for aging family members may become the best option available to more and more Americans. Eldercare can be treated as a burden, or it can be a wonderful opportunity for families.

Older parents can enjoy helping raise their grandchildren, can pick up the slack for very busy parents, can share the wisdom they have accumulated over their long lives, and can act as a bridge to previous generations, guaranteeing that you and your children share in their family history and carry it forward.

Within the marvels of sharing lives with your parents lie some very important conversations which may seem to be a breach of their privacy and compromise their independence, but they are vitally important for their care and your peace of mind. To care for your parents, you must know what you are working with, particularly in the area of advanced or long-term medical care.

This Amazing Itty Bitty® Book gives you all the information you will need to make sure that you can properly care for your parents and keep them safe and comfortable without any unpleasant surprises.

Step 1
Tough Conversation

Asking your parents or your loved ones about their retirement plan can be challenging. The following questions might be a starting point:

1. Will you be able to afford retirement?
2. Will you need financial assistance?
3. Do you want to stay by yourself or with a family member?
4. Do you have an executed will or estate plan?
5. Do you have any insurance policies in place?
6. Where can I find your financial information?
7. Do you have anything in the will that could cause friction among the family?
8. Should we or I expect an inheritance?
9. Can we or I decide where you live?
10. May I have a follow-up conversation regarding your retirement plan?

TIP: Suggestions for how to start a tough conversation:

- You must be clear about the issue.
- You must be clear about what you want to accomplish with the conversation.
- Reflect on your attitude toward the situation and your parent.
- Prepare to manage the emotions.
- Select a relaxing place.
- Plan on how to begin.
- Ask open-ended questions.
- Don't rush to fill in words, silence is perfectly okay.

No matter what is ultimately decided, remember:

- You have the best interest of your parent(s) at heart.
- Allow them to make their own decisions.
- Be sure to end the conversation on a positive note.

Step 2
Get Your Parent(s) Involved

Getting your aging parents involved in their retirement plan and their care is essential.

The following reasons explain why this is very important:

1. Your parents expect to be treated as adults with years of experience making decisions.
2. Your parents want to be respected and allowed to maintain their dignity.
3. Your parents want to keep their autonomy.
4. Your parents worked to save for retirement, and therefore have the right to be involved in all aspects of the decision-making.
5. Your parents are the ones who will have to live in any environment or situation in which they find themselves, so make sure it's the one they want, if possible.

TIP: Involving Your Parent in Their Own Care:

- Assess where they are in the aging process.
- Do not wait for a catastrophic event to have these conversations and make these important decisions.
- Ask your parents what they've put in place for themselves – trusts, Long Term Care (LTC) insurance, other.
- Ask what they will ultimately want if they find themselves unable to care for themselves.
- Involve your parents in the decision-making process.
- Allow your parent to do as much as possible with little or no assistance.
- Use indirect approaches to introducing independent activities.
- Praise every success you make as a group along this challenging path.

Early parental involvement in developing a plan of action will make things easier for them and for you in the future. Remember, do not give up.

Step 3
Gather All Important Documents

Your parents have accumulated many important documents over the years, and it is now your responsibility to proactively gather them together. Below is a list of these important documents:

1. Photo ID (Driver's License)
2. Birth certificate
3. Passport/citizenship papers
4. Divorce papers
5. Medicare/Medicaid insurance card
6. Marriage certificate
7. Credit cards
8. Mortgage documents
9. Advanced Directives
10. Legal Power of Attorney
11. Bank account information
12. Trust and loan information
13. Safe deposit box information
14. Stocks, bonds and other investment records
15. Pension documents, 401(k), and annuity contracts
16. Health Insurance Portability & Accountability (HIPPA)/Consent release of information
17. Funeral arrangement instructions
18. Other essential documents

TIP: What Will You Do Next

Gathering these essential documents is the first step toward ensuring that you have all your "ducks in a row." Next:

- Ensure these documents are accessible.
- Store documents in one master folder.
- Ensure other siblings (if any) are aware of where the documents are kept. If possible include them in these discussions.
- Ensure you obtain permission from your parents to talk with their lawyer or doctor.

Resources:

- www.aplaceformom.com/senior-care-resources/articles/living-wills-and-durable-power-of-attorney
- www.aarp.org
- www.nia.nih.gov
- www.nelf.org
- www.caringinfo.org

Step 4
Get Legal

Have a conversation about advance directives and other legal tools with your parents as soon as possible. The following are basic legal documents you should be aware of:

1. **Durable Power of Attorney (DPA)**: Grants permission to you to act on behalf of your parents.
2. **Advance Directives (AD):** Speaks for your parents when they are unable to do so.
3. **Health Care Proxy**: The person appointed to make healthcare decisions.
4. **Do Not Resuscitate/Do not intubate (DNR/DNI)**: Instructions regarding what to do in case of medical emergency.
5. **Living Will**: A document prepared in advance indicating your parents' specific desired interventions in the event they are incapacitated.
6. **Guardianship/Conservatorship**: A court-appointed conservator who will act on behalf of your parents if you cannot.

TIP: For Obtaining Legal Documents

You do not need legal representation or a lawyer to prepare or complete an Advanced Directive, Living Will or Health Proxy.

Below are free resources where you may obtain these documents:

- Caring Connections: A National Hospice and Palliative Care organization. It offers free Advanced Directives information for every state. www.caringinfo.org
- The U.S. Living Will Registry: offers links to Advanced Directive forms for each state.
  www.uslivingwillregistry.com
- MedlinePlus: U.S. National Library of Medicine is another great resource that could be of help in completing advanced directives.
  www.medlineplus.gov/advancedirectives.html

Step 5
Getting in the Game

Your parents may have been taking care of their medical affairs without you getting involved. However, as your parents age, you need to make sure you become familiar with their specialists.

Below is a list of medical specialists most often used by the elder:

1. **Cardiologist** (Heart and coronary artery)
2. **Gastroenterologist** (Stomach and digestive tract)
3. **Endocrinologist** (gland and hormone disorders)
4. **Nephrologist** (kidney)
5. **Ophthalmologist** (Eyes surgery)
6. **Pulmonary specialist** (lungs)
7. **Surgeon** (treats disease or deformities by operating on the body)
8. **Urologist** (bladder, kidney, urethra)
9. **Audiologist** – (ears)

TIP: Get the Most Out Of Every Appointment

The fact is, doctors are limited in the amount of time they spend with a patient. Preparing for each medical visit is he smart thing to do. Below are few tips to help your parents become smart consumers:

Before the appointment:

- Describe the purpose of your visit (e.g. pain, etc.).
- Put everything in writing (list questions to ask, symptoms, health concerns, etc.).
- Come with medical history and list of prescribed and over-the-counter medication.

During the visit:

- Prioritize your health concerns.
- Ask questions.
- Understand the answers.
- Request and retain copies of your parents medical records.

After the visit:

- Get advice or opinions from others.
- Manage prescriptions.
- Stay informed/educate yourself.

Step 6
Get Help Behind the Wheel

As your parents age, getting behind the wheel can become a challenge and getting them off the road can even be tougher. The following are warning signs to look for:

1. Frequently gets lost, especially within a familiar area.
2. Calling family member for directions in a familiar location.
3. Frequent car crashes, dents on garage door, curbs, etc.
4. Increased road rage and honking.
5. Difficulty concentrating and increased distraction while driving.
6. Frequent and increased number of warnings or traffic tickets.
7. Challenges checking the rear view and side mirrors while backing up.
8. Confusing gas and brake pedal.
9. Confusing traffic signals.
10. Unnecessary stops at green lights.
11. Increased driving concerns reported by neighbors and acquaintances.

TIP: Minimize the Need to Drive

Taking the key from your parents can be a challenging ordeal. Your parent wants to continue to be independent.

The following are few suggestions on how to lessen the need to drive:

- Arrange carpooling to regularly scheduled activities.
- Find private transportation providers. Uber and Lyft make this easy.
- Arrange for home delivery of prescriptions, groceries, and even meals
- Shop online for groceries and prescriptions.
- Explore "house call" physicians and other health care provider programs.
- Set-up direct deposit, automated bill payment and money transfers.
- Arrange regularly scheduled home visits by family member.

Additional resources:

- AAA Foundation for Traffic Safety: www.aaafts.org.
- Community Transportation Association of America: www.ctaa.org.
- National Highway Traffic Safety Administration: www.nhtsa.dot.gov.

Step 7
Getting a Grip on the Meds

Every year, it is reported that over **125,00** people die from taking the wrong medication, the wrong dose, taking medications that interact badly with other medications or taking medication improperly. Be aware that the risk of polypharmacy or overdose increases with age. Below are a few steps to help you get a grip on your parents' medication(s).

1. Make a list of all medications – both 'over the counter' and prescribed.
2. Ensure you know which medications your parent is taking and **why**.
3. Ensure you know the prescriber(s) of your parents' medication.
4. Ensure you know the side effects and reactions of each med.
5. Ensure you know the duration or how long it takes for your parent to complete the treatment dose (e.g. antibiotics).
6. Discard unused or expired medication.
7. Ensure you know both generic and brand names of prescribed meds.
8. Confirm with prescriber what to do in case of a missed dose.
9. Confirm other restrictions such as foods, drugs, or activities

TIP: How Much Do Your Parents Know?

To avoid overdose or preventable side effects of your parents' meds, it is important that your parent can answer the following questions:

- What medications am I taking?
- Why am I taking the medication?
- How and when should I take it?
- How will I know if it's working?
- What will happen if I refuse to take my medication?
- How long must I take the medication?
- What are the expected side effects of the medication(s)?
- What should I do in case of a medical emergency or allergic reaction?
- What food should I avoid while taking the medication?
- Can I split, crush, or dissolve the pill(s)?
- Can I mix it or take it with other medication(s)?
- How and where should I store the medicine?
- What should I do if I forget to take my medicine?

If your parents are taking many medications at different times, make a written schedule for what and when they should take each medication. Do not rely on memory.

Step 8
Encouraging Self-Care

It's often said that aging is inevitable. However, disease and disability are not. As your parents age, prevention is the secret to healthy living and self-care.

Below are a few things your parent can do to prevent disease and disability:

1. **Exercise**: Beneficial at any age.
2. **Healthy diet**: limit salt, sugar and fatty foods.
3. **Quit Smoking**: People can quit at any age.
4. **Limit alcohol**: Alcohol reduces life expectancy. Limit consumption.
5. **Safe driving**: When in doubt, ask for a ride.
6. **Monitor Your Health**: Perform an annual physical exam, including visual and hearing exam.
7. **Get enough rest**: Rest increases alertness and body rejuvenation.
8. **Nurture healthy relationships**: Makes life enjoyable and prevents depression.
9. **Stay informed**: Be aware of medical discoveries and care options.

TIP: Staying Active

One of the ways your parent can enhance self-care is by staying active. This means your parent should consider a combination of exercises for the best results.

Below are a few suggested exercises to consider:

- Brisk walking
- Jogging
- Swimming
- Aqua Aerobics
- Climbing stairs
- Dancing
- Tai Chi
- Yoga
- Meditation
- Gardening
- Weight-lifting
- Resistance bands
- Tennis
- Bowling
- Shuffle Board
- Hiking

Step 9
Finding an Adult Day/Senior Center

As your parents age, they might become lonely and less independent, even if they live with you. There are two models or types of adult day care centers.

1. Social model: offers activities only
2. Medical model: offers nursing services

Either of the models can be a welcome relief for all involved in caring for your parent.

Getting involved at an adult day/senior center can:

1. Reduce stress.
2. Decrease symptoms of depression.
3. Increase/enhances social interaction.
4. Increase activity.
5. Increase alertness.
6. Increase a sense of well-being.
7. Preserve independence.
8. Augment respite-care.
9. Augment additional health monitoring.
10. Create a routine, gives a welcome expectation of a productive day.

TIP: Adult Day Center, A Closer Look

While an adult day center offers a wide range of benefits, it is imperative that you select a center that meets your parents' needs.

Below are things you need to keep in mind before signing up:

- **Staff:** Observe how they interact with other participants.
- **Activities**: Observe if they are appropriate and stimulating.
- **Food:** Make sure you ask for a menu and check out sanitation practices.
- **Transportation:** Confirm if the center offers escorted transportation.
- **Boarding**: Ask center staff if they have a transitioning process.
- **Incontinence management**: Ask if the center manages incontinence.
- **Cost:** In addition to a daily fee, ensure there are no hidden or added fees.
- **Level of care**: Confirm the level of care provided.
- **Special needs**: Ask how they handle special needs, such as dementia or dietary restrictions.

Step 10
Limiting Stress Over Distance

At some point in your life, you will separate from your parents to pursue professional or personal interests. Whether you live a few minutes, or miles away from your aging parent, separation often causes mixed feelings of anxiety and fear.

Below are a few things you can do to minimize distress over distance:

1. Give emotional support.
2. Manage your parents' medical bills and records.
3. Schedule frequent family meetings by phone or video chat.
4. Compile and have handy your parents' medical records and the records of any legal or financial issues.
5. Research your parents' medical condition(s) and be aware of what to do if a crisis occurs.
6. Stay connected, and keep in touch with your parents' health care providers.
7. Ask your parents' friends to check in on a regular basis.
8. Seek professional help such as a geriatric care manager to organize your parents' care.

Tip: Check-In System While Away

Create systems to check on your parents and protect them which will give added support and peace of mind.

Below are a few systems you may want to consider:

- **Emergency Response Device**: Allows your parent to call for assistance.
- **Carrier Alert:** Set up an emergency Post Office phone number in case of mail accumulation.
- **Phone Alert League**: A community program to call on elderly who live alone, within a specific period of time.
- **Vial of Life Program**: Emergency data regarding your parents' health is stored in a vial in the refrigerator.
- **Friendly Visitors Programs**: Groups provide regular visits to homes.
- **Phone Reassurance Programs**: Daily call by a network system to check on your parent.
- **Remote Patient Monitoring**: Daily monitoring of vital signs. Patient's contact individual receives a call if there is no data entered.

Step 11
Anticipating Your Parents' Needs

As your parents age, the need for support increases. The following are signs that additional support is needed:

- **Basic tasks**: Challenges with dressing, cooking, climbing, managing medications, and so on.
- **Hygiene:** Sloppy appearance, foul body and/or mouth odor.
- **Health:** Unexplained weight loss, incontinence, excessive sleepiness.
- **Responsibilities**: Unpaid bills, unopened mail, unfilled prescriptions, etc.
- **Cognitive functions**: Increased forgetfulness, loss of reasoning skills, forgetting familiar peoples' names.
- **Attitude**: Unusual display of verbal or physical abuse, paranoia and depression.
- **Apathy**: Lack of interest in hobbies, disinterest in socializing.
- **Isolated living conditions**: Limited access to transportation – living alone.

TIP: Your Parents' Activity Inventory

As soon as you see these changes, it is important to figure out what your parents can or cannot do.

The following tips will help you to assess your parents' daily living activities:

Instrumental daily living activities to monitor:

- Grocery shopping
- Getting around the house
- Making and answering calls
- Cooking for themselves
- Managing money
- Keeping track of medications

Activities of daily living:

- Bathing
- Dressing
- Grooming
- Use of toilet
- Feeding themselves
- Getting in and out of bed
- Self-administering medication

Step 12
Anticipating the Cost of Care

Caring for your loved one at home comes with a cost, directly and indirectly. Below are a few costs you should prepare for.

1. Transportation
2. Medication (not covered by insurance)
3. Medical bills
4. Special diet (diabetes, etc.)
5. Non-breakable glasses and dishware
6. Assistive devices (e.g. Wheelchair)
7. Home modification
8. Fixtures (handrails, etc.)
9. Private duty assistant
10. Loss of income
11. Loss of time (personal and work)
12. Loss of independence
13. Lost wages due to caring for parent
14. Emergency medical response button
15. Housing (rent)
16. Clothes and footwear
17. Hearing aids
18. Dental care

TIP: Preparing for Unexpected Expenses

Develop a family plan to cover your loved one's care costs. Below are a few tips to explore:

- Ask your employer if they offer long-term care insurance to employees and their family.
- Open a dedicated savings and checking account for your parents' expenditures.
- Initiate conversation with your family regarding a reimbursement policy.
- Reevaluate your parents' financial needs every three- to six-months.
- Discuss sharing responsibilities with other family members.

Below are tips on how to reduce your parents' living expenses:

- Consider ways to scale down your parents' living quarters.
- Buy low-maintenance products.
- Use money-saving coupons.
- If they have more than one car, keep one car and sell the other.
- Limit impulse purchases.
- Ask for loan, mortgage and insurance payment waivers.
- Ask for seniors' discounts.
- Buy sale items.
- Check bills for errors and overcharges.

Step 13
Long-Term Care: Where Is the Money?

Caring for dependent elderly parents over a sustained period – usually six months or more – is considered long-term care. It covers a range of services and support for your parents' personal care needs.

Below are a few questions you need to consider when your parents need long-term care:

1. What is your parents' long-term financial picture?
2. How much can my parents and I afford?
3. How much am I willing to spend personally?
4. What types of services does long-term care provide?
5. What is the most common type of long-term care?
6. How long does long-term care last?
7. How can I tell if my parents need long-term care?
8. Who provides long-term care in their home?
9. What are the various options to pay for long-term care?
10. Does Medicare or Medicaid pay for long-term care?
11. Is long-term care insurance optional?

TIP: Who Pays for Long-Term Care?

Paying for long-term care can be quite expensive. It is important to know who pays for what and then figure out your options.

Below are a few payer sources to consider:

- **Medicare**: Pays for acute care or short-term hospital or rehab care.
- **Medigap**: Pays for expenses that Medicare will not cover.
- **Medicaid**: For low income. Pays for long-term care, but must *spend down* to qualify.
- **Long-term care insurance**: Specific to LTC living and other expenses.
- **Reverse Mortgage**: Receive cash for the equity of a home.
- **Veteran's Benefits**: Helps veterans pay for personal and long-term care.
- **Annuities**: Two types; immediate and deferred long-term annuities. Both pay for long-term care.
- **Personal fund**: Paying for long-term care out-of-pocket.

Step 14
Adding Life to Years

Aging is a normal process. It is a process that entails accumulating wisdom, experience, and memories. You can add life to years (not years to life) by asking your parent(s) the questions such as:

1. What interests you the most now?
2. What is most important to you right now?
3. Where can you get information about things that are important to you?
4. Is there anything you would like to explore?
5. Where can you get information on what you want to explore?
6. Is there any specific place you would like to volunteer or visit?
7. Is there any unfulfilled dream you would like to pursue?
8. Is there any strained relationship you would like to restore?
9. Is there anyone you would like to meet or talk with?
10. At the end of your life, how do you want to be remembered?

TIP: Cultivate a New Interest

As your parents age, they may experience a change in priorities and interests. It is important that you support and encourage new activities or hobbies for your parents.

Below are a few activities you might explore:

- Volunteering
- Playing a musical instrument
- Handicrafts and sewing
- Fitness and mall-walking
- Stamp and coin collections
- Games and puzzles
- Singing and dancing
- Teaching
- Engaging in religious activities
- Creative writing and letter writing
- Acting and modeling
- Reading and storytelling
- Cooking and baking
- Traveling and vacationing
- Painting and drawing
- Outings to parks, museums, and other places of interest

Step 15
Keep the Ability in Disability

When your parents can no longer care for themselves or become disabled, this can be very stressful for all parties involved.

Take a moment to look at things from their perspectives.

It is important to know that living with disability does not necessarily mean living with sickness.

A few things to consider:

1. Keep yourself informed about access to health professionals and other resources.
2. Learn what is curable, treatable, and correctible.
3. Be prepared and make room for your parents' mixed emotions.
4. Celebrate and acknowledge your parents' accomplishments, even with disabilities.
5. Be sure to ask for and accept help from others.
6. Avoid blaming yourself or others for your parents' condition.
7. Stay physically, emotionally, and mentally strong.

TIP: Taking the Time to Breathe

Caring for aging parents, especially if disabled, can be stressful, time-consuming, and costly.

It is imperative that you take time to breathe. Reflect on wins, not losses. Maximize quality of life for yourself and parents. Find ways to spend more relaxing time with them.

Below are a few things or activities to make the moment memorable:

- **Stay Connected**: Visit frequently by phone or video chat.
- **Complement each other**: Celebrate all family achievements and accomplishments.
- **Forgive and let go**: Make room for weakness, failures, and ignore mistakes.
- **Family history**: Explore, learn, and share family history and heritage.
- **Draw a family tree**: Create a chart that shows how family members are related.
- **Plan family reunion**: Encourage extended family ties.
- **Take pictures**: Capture memorable events.
- **Exchange photo albums**: Label pictures

You've finished. Before you go…

Tweet/share that you finished this book.

Please star rate this book.

Reviews are solid gold to writers. Please take a few minutes to give us some itty bitty feedback.

ABOUT THE AUTHOR

John Smith is the founder of Prestige Healthcare Resources (PHR) DBA Personnel Results, an in-home care, case management, and staffing agency, which focuses on improving the lifestyles of the elderly and senior population.

He came to the United States as an immigrant. For several years before that move, he experienced several painful experiences and setbacks, the roughest being a ten-year period of living in Liberia, where he endured exposure to a ravaging civil war. Some misfortune continued after he reached the U.S.; while working at a menial job, he almost lost a finger in a "near miss" incident.

Despite these and other set-backs, Mr. Smith was determined to succeed as the voice for the vulnerable elderly population and to be the best in what he does. Hence, his nickname "**No Excuse Guy**" is not a coincidence.

After graduating with a bachelor of science degree in nursing, Mr. Smith went on to work at various hospital settings in a variety of specialties. He worked as a Telemetry Nurse, Medical/Surgical Nurse, Operating Room Nurse, Psychiatric Nurse, Hospice Nurse, Home Health Nurse and Community Health Nurse. Despite working at various health care settings and specialties, his true love and passion is giving voice to the elderly population.

While working in the health care industry, Mr. Smith noticed several disparities, which fueled his desire to found Prestige Healthcare Resources in 2009 with the objective of enhancing and improving the lifestyle of the elderly population and their families.

Under his leadership, Prestige expanded into five states and became one of the prime case management companies in the District of Columbia. The Prestige teams, under the supervision of Mr. Smith, organically grew the company from a couple of elderly patients to almost six hundred.

Mr. Smith has been invited to speak on numerous occasions to tell his story and offer much-needed advice to individuals and families on how to keep their loved ones safe at home. He has helped countless families learn how to reduce unnecessary hospital readmissions and prevent full-time institutionalization. He has been an inspirational icon for the healthcare industry, frequently offering his expertise to new employees, students, and people up and down the corporate ladder.

Outside of work, Mr. Smith enjoys spending time with his family, working out, playing tennis, ping-pong, and volleyball.

He can be reached at www.prestigewecare.com

If you liked this Amazing Itty Bitty® Book you might also enjoy:

- **Your Amazing Itty Bitty® Cancer Book** – Jacqueline Kreple

- **Your Amazing Itty Bitty® Staying Young At Any Age Book** – Dianna Whitley

- **Your Amazing Itty Bitty® Senior Sexuality Book** – Randy and Rev. Jenny Dickason

Or many more Itty Bitty® books available online.

www.ingramcontent.com/pod-product-compliance
Lightning Source LLC
Chambersburg PA
CBHW061304040426
42444CB00010B/2510